AGS *American Literature*
Student Workbook

by
Molly Harrington Dugan

AGS®

American Guidance Service, Inc.
Circle Pines, Minnesota 55014-1796
1-800-328-2560

ISBN 0-7854-1882-2

Product Number 93003

A 0 9 8 7 6 5 4

Table of Contents

Historical Background

Part A Directions The following information is taken from the Historical Background of Unit 1. Place each event in correct time sequence. Write the letter of the first event after item 1, the letter of the second event after item 2, and so on.

1. _____   **a.** Colonists established plantations in the South.

2. _____   **b.** A distinctive style of literature emerged with the works of Edgar Allan Poe and Washington Irving.

3. _____   **c.** Conflict between England and the colonies came to a head.

4. _____   **d.** The Puritans traveled to America to seek religious freedom.

5. _____   **e.** Enslaved Africans were brought to America.

6. _____   **f.** American Indians established early civilizations in America.

7. _____   **g.** The American Revolution brought about a new government in America.

8. _____   **h.** Transportation began to develop toward the West between 1790 and 1830.

Part B Directions Answer the following questions in complete sentences. Write your answers on the lines provided.

1. Early American literature was very practical. What four types of writing were common during this period?

_____

_____

_____

2. How were the works of Poe and Irving significant to American history?

_____

_____

_____

The History of Plymouth Plantation

Directions Write *True* if the statement is true; write *False* if the statement is not true. Write your answer on the line provided before each statement. If the statement is false, draw a line through the error and write the correct word or words below that statement.

_____ **1.** The Pilgrims arrived on the *Mayflower.*

    _____

_____ **2.** These Pilgrims came to America to seek economic freedom.

    _____

_____ **3.** The Pilgrims feared they would find wild beasts and fierce men in this new land.

    _____

_____ **4.** The ship landed on the shore of territory that is now Maryland.

    _____

_____ **5.** The Pilgrims came in the winter of 1620.

    _____

_____ **6.** As soon as they landed, the men and women fell to their knees and thanked God for their safe arrival.

    _____

_____ **7.** The ocean they crossed had been small and smooth.

    _____

_____ **8.** The Pilgrims had come from Italy.

    _____

_____ **9.** William Bradford was one of the Pilgrims.

    _____

_____ **10.** The settlers described the land as a fierce, desolate wilderness.

    _____

To My Dear and Loving Husband

Directions Read the following statements. Choose the letter of the answer that best completes each statement about "To My Dear and Loving Husband." Write your answer on the line provided before each statement.

_____ 1. This selection, "To My Dear and Loving Husband," is an example of a _____.
 a. play **b.** short story **c.** speech **d.** poem

_____ 2. Anne Bradstreet tells only of her _____ in this work.
 a. love for her husband **b.** love for her country
 c. unhappiness about her new life **d.** anger about her children

_____ 3. Anne Bradstreet believes that she and her husband _____.
 a. should separate **b.** will never get along
 c. should divorce **d.** love each other

_____ 4. "To My Dear and Loving Husband" has _____.
 a. a rhyming pattern **b.** no rhyme
 c. many lines of specific details **d.** none of the above

_____ 5. This poem was written in approximately _____.
 a. 1960 **b.** 1800 **c.** 1865 **d.** 1640

_____ 6. This selection was later published in _____.
 a. London **b.** Rome **c.** Paris **d.** Boston

_____ 7. In this selection, Anne Bradstreet indicates that she believes in _____.
 a. the Revolutionary War **b.** an afterlife
 c. happiness **d.** education

_____ 8. The author compares her love with _____.
 a. fruit **b.** riches and gold
 c. war **d.** diamonds

_____ 9. Anne Bradstreet also gives information about _____ in this selection.
 a. her children **b.** America
 c. her church **d.** none of the above

_____ 10. Anne Bradstreet seems to be _____.
 a. depressed **b.** lonely **c.** powerful **d.** content

Poor Richard's Almanac

Directions   Complete the following chart about *Poor Richard's Almanac*. Add information about Benjamin Franklin and the almanac that he published. Write your answers in the spaces provided in each case.

Personal Information about Benjamin Franklin
1. Date of birth
2. Place of birth
3. Number of children in his family
4. First known work
5. In 1729 Franklin produced
6. A scientific accomplishment
7. Accomplishment as a statesman
8. Died in the year

Publishing Information about *Poor Richard's Almanac*
9. Date introduced
10. Definition of almanac
11. Franklin used the pseudonym
12. Published until
13. Popular because
14. Definition of aphorism
15. Profitable because

The American Crisis, Number 1

Directions Write *True* if the statement is true; write *False* if the statement is not true. Write your answer on the line provided before each statement. Then if the statement is false, correct it by writing the true fact on the line provided below that statement.

_____ **1.** Thomas Paine came to the United States representing the British government.

_____

_____ **2.** When Paine's writing was read to troops before the Battle of Trenton, it helped improve their mood.

_____

_____ **3.** Paine writes that England had a right to exert power over the colonies.

_____

_____ **4.** Paine writes that God will not abandon people with such a good cause.

_____

_____ **5.** According to Paine, Voltaire, a French writer, believes that King William was never strong.

_____

_____ **6.** *Relinquish* means "to fortify."

_____

_____ **7.** Paine writes that perseverance and fortitude are most important.

_____

_____ **8.** Paine feels the colonists can win despite George Washington's weaknesses.

_____

_____ **9.** Paine did not describe the possible consequences of a British victory.

_____

_____ **10.** In 1809, Thomas Paine died a very wealthy man.

_____

Wouter Van Twiller

Part A Directions   Write *True* if the statement is true; write *False* if the
statement is not true. Write your answer on the line provided
before each statement. If the statement is false, correct it by
writing the true fact on the line below the statement.

_____   **1.** "Wouter Van Twiller" is a work of fiction.

_____

_____   **2.** Washington Irving was a writer of the twentieth century.

_____

_____   **3.** This story is an example of satire.

_____

_____   **4.** Wouter Van Twiller is an excellent president.

_____

_____   **5.** Wouter Van Twiller works very hard.

_____

_____   **6.** Wouter Van Twiller has a vague, unfurrowed face.

_____

_____   **7.** Wouter Van Twiller is five feet six inches tall and six feet five inches wide.

_____

_____   **8.** People often believed that Wouter was deep in thought.

_____

_____   **9.** This story suggests that some people are easily impressed by elected officials.

_____

_____   **10.** Van Twiller's name translates to the Doubter.

_____

Wouter Van Twiller, continued

_____**11.** The author suggests that some dumb animals, like the owl, are credited with intelligence.

_____

_____**12.** Wouter Van Twiller loved a good joke.

_____

_____**13.** Wouter Van Twiller always ate three meals a day and slept eight hours a day.

_____

_____**14.** Wouter Van Twiller had a head like a perfect square.

_____

_____**15.** Wouter Van Twiller sometimes made guttural sounds that people believed were the sounds of his "doubts and opinions."

_____

Part B Directions   Reread the portion of the story that details the appearance of Wouter Van Twiller. List his physical characteristics on the lines below. Then, in the space provided, draw a picture of this character.

Wouter Van Twiller

1. Height: _____

2. Size around: _____

3. Head shape: _____

4. Body shape and legs: _____

5. Facial features: _____

American Indian Poetry

Directions Each statement below could be made about some group of American Indians. Read each statement. On the line before each statement write *S* if it could be said of the Sioux, *O* if it could be said of the Omaha, *C* for Chippewa, or *A* for all three.

1. _____ Some of them were Tetons.

2. _____ They were also called Ojibwa.

3. _____ They lived in what is now Nebraska.

4. _____ They were in America before the Europeans came.

5. _____ The mood of their poem is peaceful.

6. _____ They wanted control of the rice lands.

7. _____ Their poems were originally chants, songs, or speeches.

8. _____ Identifying with animals is apparent in their poem.

9. _____ Big Elk belonged to this group.

10. _____ They hunted buffalo.

11. _____ Their poem refers to a Supreme Being.

12. _____ In their poetry, they discuss life and death.

13. _____ Black Buffalo was one of their leaders.

14. _____ They lived near the Great Lakes.

15. _____ The mood of their poem is one of quiet wisdom.

The Origin of Plumage

Many myths are hundreds of years old; they attempt to explain how things in the natural world came to be. A myth often uses personification, a literary device that gives to nonhuman beings the characteristics of a human. For example, the birds in "The Origin of Plumage" can reason, talk, and make decisions. Because myths are passed down by word of mouth, they allow a teller to change parts of the story as it is retold.

Directions Listed below are four titles of myths similar to "The Origin of Plumage." Think about the unique characteristics of the animal described in each title. How might this unusual trait become a characteristic of that animal? How might this trait be a help to that animal? Write an original myth for one of the four titles suggested below. If you wish, create your own title. Use personification in your story; make your main animal character talk and think like a human. Remember to use a new paragraph and quotation marks every time a character speaks.

Sample Titles

How the Turtle's Shell Was Formed

Why the Skunk Developed an Odor

How the Bear Lost Its Tail

How the Rattlesnake Got Its Rattle

_____

_____

_____

_____

_____

_____

The Black Cat

Part A Directions   Read the following statements about "The Black Cat." Choose the best answer to complete each statement. Write your answer on the line provided below each statement.

1. Edgar Allan Poe usually wrote of (humorous events, horrid and frightening events).

_____

2. "The Black Cat" is told in the (first person, third person).

_____

3. The storyteller mentions that in his childhood he (loved, hated) animals.

_____

4. The man in the story killed the first cat by (shooting, hanging) him.

_____

5. After the house burned in a fire, everyone could see the figure of a (cat, man) on one wall.

_____

6. The man brought home a second black cat that he grew to (love, hate).

_____

7. The man killed his wife with (an axe, a gun).

_____

8. The man buried his wife in (a graveyard, the basement).

_____

9. The second cat (disappeared, was killed) after the wife was murdered.

_____

10. The cat's howl helped the police find the (wife's body, murder weapon).

_____

The Black Cat, continued

The order in which an author arranges incidents or events in a story is called the plot structure. Read about these five parts of plot structure.

1. The **introduction** gives the reader information necessary for understanding a story. It introduces characters and setting.

2. The **rising action** is the longest part of most stories. Conflicts are introduced and may become complicated. The reader is kept in suspense as to how they will be resolved.

3. The **climax** is the turning point of a story. It is the point at which a character takes some action that will lead either to a tragic or happy ending.

4. The **falling action** follows the climax. Complications are explained to the reader, who now has an idea of how the story will turn out. However, sometimes an author will include a final moment of suspense, and things may not go the way that they seem to be going.

5. The **conclusion** ends the story and makes all loose ends of the plot clear to the reader.

Part B Directions   Chart the plot structure of "The Black Cat." Identify each statement below as *Introduction, Rising Action, Climax, Falling Action,* or *Conclusion.* Write your answers on the lines provided. Note that the statements are not listed in the order in which events actually occurred in the story.

_____ 1. The house burns down.

_____ 2. The narrator describes his childhood and marriage.

_____ 3. The howling cat leads the police to discover the wife's body.

_____ 4. The narrator explains that he is going to tell his story.

_____ 5. Aiming to kill the cat, the narrator murders his wife.

_____ 6. The narrator's drinking increases.

_____ 7. The narrator acquires a second cat.

_____ 8. The narrator decides to bury his wife's body in the cellar wall.

_____ 9. The narrator tortures and kills Pluto.

_____ 10. The neighbors discover the image of a cat at the wall.

Annabel Lee

Directions   Refer to the poem "Annabel Lee" to complete each important line
from this poem by Edgar Allan Poe. Write the missing words on the
line provided in each case.

1. "And this maiden she lived with no other thought

   Than _____."

2. "I was a child and _____"

3. "But we loved with a love that was _____"

4. "So that her highborn kinsmen came

   And _____"

5. "The angels, not half so happy in heaven,

   Went _____"

6. "That the wind came out of the cloud by night,

   Chilling and _____."

7. "For the moon never beams, without bringing me dreams

   Of _____"

8. "And so, all the night tide, I _____"

9. "Of my darling—my darling—my life and _____"

10. "In her sepulchre there by the sea—

    In her _____."

Unit 1 Review

Part A Directions Review the Historical Background and timeline for Unit 1. Identify the event that occurred on each date. Write your answers.

1. 1620_____

2. 1630_____

3. 1650_____

4. 1732_____

5. 1775_____

6. 1776_____

7. 1783_____

8. 1812_____

9. 1819_____

10. 1844_____

Part B Directions Identify the genre, or form of literature, for each work. Write the letters of the correct genres on the lines provided. Some answers will be used more than once.

_____ **1.** *The History of Plymouth Plantation*   **a.** poem

_____ **2.** "The Origin of Plumage"   **b.** pamphlet

_____ **3.** "The Black Cat"   **c.** collection

_____ **4.** "Wouter Van Twiller"   **d.** character sketch

_____ **5.** "To My Dear and Loving Husband"   **e.** short story

_____ **6.** Omaha quotation   **f.** diary

_____ **7.** Sayings of Poor Richard   **g.** aphorisms

_____ **8.** *The American Crisis, Number 1*   **h.** myth

_____ **9.** "Annabel Lee"   **i.** speech

_____ **10.** *The Tenth Muse Lately Sprung up in America*

Unit 1 Review, continued

Part C Directions   Read the names of American Indian groups and individual authors listed below. Write one fact about the life of each of these groups or individuals.

1. Omaha _____

_____

2. Chippewa _____

_____

3. Sioux _____

_____

4. William Bradford _____

_____

5. Anne Bradstreet _____

_____

6. Thomas Paine _____

_____

7. Benjamin Franklin _____

_____

8. Washington Irving _____

_____

9. Edgar Allan Poe _____

_____

10. Richard Saunders _____

_____

Historical Background

Directions   Answer the following questions about the Historical Background to
Unit 2. Write your answers in complete sentences.

1. What period of time is represented in this unit?

_____

2. What were four developments in transportation during this period?

_____

3. What did the "age of industry" give the common person?

_____

4. What were three unhappy aspects of the industrialization of the North?

_____

5. What types of people were being drawn to the antislavery cause?

_____

6. What is transcendentalism?

_____

_____

7. What important comment could be made about New England during this period?

_____

8. What did Thoreau and Emerson have in common, in terms of their writing?

_____

9. Name the five New England romantics represented in this unit.

_____

10. Identify one work for each of the writers that you have listed.

_____

_____

American Literature

Self-Reliance

Part A Directions   Listed below are several phrases. Write *Yes* for the ideas that were discussed in the work "Self-Reliance." Write *No* for the ideas that were not discussed in Emerson's essay. Write your answers on the lines provided.

_____   **1.** Believe your own thought.

_____   **2.** Envy is ignorance.

_____   **3.** A person must take himself for better or for worse.

_____   **4.** Live and let live.

_____   **5.** Life is full of surprises.

_____   **6.** Trust thyself.

_____   **7.** Invest your money wisely.

_____   **8.** Be prepared to defend your country.

_____   **9.** Speak what you think now.

_____   **10.** Look to others for guidance.

_____   **11.** Imitation is more rewarding than envy.

_____   **12.** Insist on yourself.

_____   **13.** Good friends always think alike.

_____   **14.** Nothing can bring you peace but yourself.

_____   **15.** Greed is an evil thing.

Part B Directions   Review the statements for which you listed *Yes* in Part A above. Recall Ralph Waldo Emerson's ideas concerning self-reliance. Think about someone you know or have heard about who has shown self-reliance in such a positive way. In a few sentences, describe how this person demonstrated self-reliance. Write your answer in complete sentences on the lines provided.

_____

_____

_____

Walden

Directions Answer the following questions. Write your answers
in complete sentences.

1. What did the author mean by the "experiment" that he referred to in the beginning of this essay?

   _____

2. On what date did the author move to the woods? Why was that date significant?

   _____

3. What did Thoreau's cabin look like?

   _____

4. What did the wind do for Thoreau?

   _____

5. What kind of birds did Thoreau consider his neighbors?

   _____

6. Where was Walden Pond located?

   _____

7. What were some views visible to Thoreau?

   _____

8. For what length of time did Thoreau live in the woods?

   _____

9. From what point of view is this story told?

   _____

10. What might be another appropriate title for this work?

   _____

Dr. Heidegger's Experiment

Part A Directions   Complete the following chart about "Dr. Heidegger's Experiment." Identify the elements of fiction by writing the correct information in the spaces provided.

1. Title and Author	
2. Genre (poem, short story, novel, play, etc.)	
3. Main Character	
4. Supporting Characters	
5. Unseen Character (referred to but not present)	
6. Setting: Place	
7. Setting: Time	
8. Mood (main emotion)	
9. Plot	
10. Theme or Moral	

Dr. Heidegger's Experiment, continued

Part B Directions   Determine the structure of "Dr. Heidegger's Experiment." Identify each statement below as *Introduction, Rising Action, Climax, Falling Action,* or *Conclusion.* Write your answers on the lines provided. Note that the statements are not listed in the order in which events actually occurred in the story.

_____   **1.** The guests drink the fluid.

_____   **2.** The guests resolve to move to Florida to drink from the Fountain of Youth.

_____   **3.** The guests gather in the study of Dr. Heidegger.

_____   **4.** Dr. Heidegger explains why he brought them together.

_____   **5.** The rose comes to life when dropped in the fluid.

_____   **6.** The guests grow young.

_____   **7.** The guests grow old again.

_____   **8.** The vase of fluid crashes to the floor and breaks.

Part C Directions   Match each name with the correct description of that character. Write the letters of your answers on the lines provided.

_____   **1.** Widow Wycherly

_____   **2.** Mr. Gascoigne

_____   **3.** Mr. Medbourne

_____   **4.** Dr. Heidegger

_____   **5.** Colonel Killigrew

_____   **6.** Sylvia Ward

_____   **7.** Ponce de Leon

a. wanted to conduct an experiment

b. dies on the bridal evening

c. wished to be beautiful again

d. was a merchant who had lost all his money

e. was a ruined politician

f. ruined his health by pursuing sinful pleasures

g. explored Florida

The Fiddler

Directions   Read the following quotations from "The Fiddler." Think about the meaning of the underlined word in each case. On the line provided before each statement, write the letter of the word or phrase that is nearest in meaning to the underlined word.

_____ 1. ". . . enthusiastic <u>throngs</u> were crowding to a circus."
     a. children   **b.** masses of people
     c. small groups   **d.** famous people

_____ 2. "Presently my old friend Standard rather <u>boisterously</u> accosted me."
     a. loudly   **b.** meekly
     c. softly   **d.** surprisingly

_____ 3. "Without having time or inclination to resent so <u>mortifying</u> a mistake."
     a. small   **b.** genuine
     c. humorous   **d.** embarrassing

_____ 4. ". . . claps, thumps, deafening huzzas; the vast assembly seemed frantic with <u>acclamation</u>."
     a. quiet attention   **b.** disapproval
     c. criticism   **d.** applause

_____ 5. "Though greatly <u>subdued</u> from its former hilarity, his face still shone with gladness."
     a. reduced   **b.** increased
     c. saddened   **d.** angered

_____ 6. "Suddenly remembering an <u>engagement</u>, he took up his hat, bowed pleasantly, and left us."
     a. luncheon   **b.** party
     c. marriage   **d.** meeting

_____ 7. "This last remark set me to <u>pondering</u> again."
     a. eating   **b.** thinking
     c. talking   **d.** applauding

_____ 8. "I don't say I <u>scorn</u> him; you are unjust. I simply declare that his is no pattern for me."
     a. admire   **b.** adore
     c. regard with contempt   **d.** pity

_____ 9. ". . . I was transfixed by something miraculously <u>superior</u> in the style."
     a. excellent   **b.** superb
     c. above all others   **d.** all of the above

_____ 10. "Next day I tore all my <u>manuscripts</u>, bought me a fiddle, and went to take regular lessons of Hautboy."
     a. magazines   **b.** school books
     c. records   **d.** writings

Shiloh

Part A Directions Read "Shiloh" in your textbook. Then, match each noun from Column A with the word that describes it from Column B. Write the letters of the correct answers on the lines provided.

Column A

_____ **1.** swallows

_____ **2.** days

_____ **3.** rain

_____ **4.** groan

_____ **5.** church

_____ **6.** foeman

_____ **7.** fight

_____ **8.** prayer

Column B

a. Sunday

b. lone

c. April

d. skimming

e. natural

f. parting

g. dying

h. clouded

Part B Directions Read the groups of words below. Choose one word from each group that belongs in the poem "Shiloh." Write the correct word on the line provided.

1. field—desert—prairie _____

2. cabin—schoolhouse—church _____

3. pain—health—victory _____

4. stone—brick—log-built _____

5. whispered—hushed—loud _____

6. bullet—cannon—rifle _____

7. clever—parched—wicked _____

American Literature

Poems by Emily Dickinson

Directions Read the following statements about the poetry of Emily Dickinson. Write *True* if the statement is true; write *False* if the statement is not true. Write your answers on the lines provided.

The Poetry of Emily Dickinson

_____   **1.** Many of Emily Dickinson's poems were about death.

_____   **2.** Emily Dickinson's poetry never rhymed.

_____   **3.** Emily Dickinson used symbols in her poems.

"Because I could not stop for Death"

_____   **4.** In this poem, death is represented by a carriage driver.

_____   **5.** In this poem, the driver is seen as evil.

_____   **6.** In this poem, the rider is afraid of being killed.

_____   **7.** The ride in the carriage is pleasant and slow.

_____   **8.** The carriage passed by a school and a field.

_____   **9.** As the sun set, the air grew colder.

"I never saw a moor"

_____   **10.** The poet describes her visit to the seashore in this poem.

_____   **11.** The tone of this poem is very sad and depressing.

_____   **12.** This poem suggests that the author believes in God and heaven.

"My life closed twice before its close"

_____   **13.** According to this poem, the author has experienced two partings so far in her life.

_____   **14.** In this poem, the author feels hopeless about parting from a lover.

_____   **15.** In this poem, the author states that love for a child is beautiful.

Unit 2 Review

Part A Directions Reread the Historical Background and timeline for Unit 2. Complete the following statements by adding the correct dates. Write your answers on the lines provided.

1. The Golden Age of New England began in the _____.

2. Ralph Waldo Emerson published "Self-Reliance" in the year _____.

3. The book about Thoreau's two years of life alone by a pond was published in _____.

4. "Dr. Heidegger's Experiment" by Nathaniel Hawthorne was published in _____.

5. _____ was the year in which the California Gold Rush began.

Part B Directions Identify the correct author for each of the statements below. In each case, write the last name of the author on the line provided. The names of some authors will be used more than once.

_____ 1. I moved to the country to live a simple life.

_____ 2. I was born in Amherst, Massachusetts.

_____ 3. I wrote about the importance of an independent spirit in "Self-Reliance."

_____ 4. My ancestors participated in the Salem witch trials during the 1690s.

_____ 5. I was an adventurer who was drawn to the sea.

_____ 6. I rarely left my father's house.

_____ 7. I wrote *The Scarlet Letter*.

_____ 8. I published my essays in 1854.

_____ 9. I wrote many poems about death and an afterlife.

_____ 10. I wrote the poem "Shiloh."

Unit 2 Review, continued

Part C Directions   A theme is the statement of the main idea expressed in a literary work. Complete the theme statement for each of the following selections.

Example: "I never saw a moor"
One does not have to see heaven to believe in it.

1. "Self-Reliance"

One should _____

_____

2. *Walden*

Living close to nature _____

_____

3. "Dr. Heidegger's Experiment"

Some people _____

_____

4. "The Fiddler"

Success _____

_____

_____

_____

5. "Shiloh"

War _____

_____

_____

Historical Background

Directions   Read the statements below. Choose the letter of the item that best completes each statement. Write your answer on the line provided before each statement.

_____ 1. The Civil War began in the year _____.
- **a.** 1865
- **b.** 1965
- **c.** 1900
- **d.** 1861

_____ 2. The man who held the office of President of the United States during the Civil War was _____.
- **a.** Abraham Lincoln
- **b.** John Kennedy
- **c.** John Adams
- **d.** George Washington

_____ 3. The Civil War began at _____.
- **a.** Walden Pond
- **b.** Fort Sumter
- **c.** the Chisholm Trail
- **d.** the Mississippi River

_____ 4. The period of building after the Civil War was known as _____.
- **a.** Aftermath
- **b.** Problem Control
- **c.** War Rebuilding
- **d.** Reconstruction

_____ 5. During this period, more and more American Indians were forced _____.
- **a.** to live on reservations
- **b.** to live in Boston
- **c.** eastward
- **d.** into slavery

_____ 6. Literature about the _____ person became popular after the Civil War.
- **a.** aristocratic
- **b.** wealthy
- **c.** common
- **d.** well-educated

_____ 7. The new direction in literature during this time was called _____.
- **a.** traditional
- **b.** transcendentalist
- **c.** classic
- **d.** local color

_____ 8. Local color was represented by _____.
- **a.** the way people spoke
- **b.** the way people behaved
- **c.** local customs
- **d.** all of the above

_____ 9. A speech by _____ expresses the hopes that African Americans have the right to vote.
- **a.** Mark Twain
- **b.** Walt Whitman
- **c.** Frederick Douglass
- **d.** Abraham Lincoln

_____ 10. Chief Seattle's speech expresses sadness because American Indians have _____.
- **a.** lost the Civil War
- **b.** moved to South Carolina
- **c.** traveled on the Mississippi
- **d.** lost their land

Thirty-Five

Directions Write *True* if the statement is true; write *False* if the statement is not true. Write your answer on the line provided before each statement. Then, if the statement is false, correct it by writing the true fact on the line provided below that statement.

_____ **1.** When Sarah Josepha Hale wrote "Thirty-Five," she was sixty-one years old.

_____

_____ **2.** This poem did not appeal to women.

_____

_____ **3.** The author of this poem was also once the editor of *Godey's Lady's Book*.

_____

_____ **4.** Sarah Josepha Hale also wrote "Mary Had a Little Lamb."

_____

_____ **5.** In this poem, the author mentions how awful it is to grow old.

_____

_____ **6.** The author says that a rose is sweeter when the bloom has passed.

_____

_____ **7.** The author would keep each link in "Memory's gold chain."

_____

_____ **8.** The author of this poem seems to have had a very difficult and unhappy life.

_____

_____ **9.** This poem appeared in 1849.

_____

_____ **10.** The language of this poem was meant to be taken literally.

_____

Spirituals

Part A Directions Match the word or phrase in Column A with its description in Column B. Write the letters of your answers on the lines provided.

Column A

_____ 1. spirituals

_____ 2. heaven

_____ 3. plantations

_____ 4. enslaved Africans

_____ 5. refrain

Column B

a. those who made up these songs of hope

b. where these songs were originally sung

c. the songs of hope sung by slaves and plantation workers

d. words or lines that are repeated for emphasis

e. "home," "promised land," or "Campground"

Part B Directions Review the information given in your text about "Swing Low, Sweet Chariot" and "Deep River." Read the two songs. Then, complete the following chart about these two spirituals. Write your answers in the spaces provided.

	"Swing Low, Sweet Chariot"	"Deep River"
1. Author		
2. Does the spiritual contain rhyme?		
3. One example of dialect		
4. Four examples of religious references		
5. Refrain		

The Fugitive Blacksmith

Part A Directions   Read the following events from *The Fugitive Blacksmith*. Place these events in the correct order. Write the letter of the first event after 1, the letter of the second event after 2, and so on. The first event has already been listed for you.

1. __b__   **a.** The author uses the North Star as his guide.

2. _____   **b.** The author takes some bread for his journey.

3. _____   **c.** The author passes a tollgate and learns that he has reached Pennsylvania.

4. _____   **d.** The author struggles with his captors, who drag him into the tavern.

5. _____   **e.** The author is invited into the home of W. W., a Quaker, who feeds and helps him.

6. _____   **f.** The author goes through the woods and begins his escape to freedom.

7. _____   **g.** After escaping from his captors, the author hopes he may be near free soil.

8. _____   **h.** On the first day out, the author hides in a corn shock.

9. _____   **i.** On the third day, a young man asks the author if he has free papers.

10. _____   **j.** The author tells the tale of a slave trader and slaves who died from the smallpox.

Part B Directions   Match the following characters from *The Fugitive Blacksmith* with the comments thought or said by each person. Write the letters of your answers on the lines provided.

_____   **1.** "... you should not travel on this road: you will be taken up before you have gone three miles."

_____   **2.** "I will see then if you don't stop, you black rascal."

_____   **3.** "What substance is there in a piece of dry Indian-bread?"

_____   **4.** "Come in and take thy breakfast, and get warm ..."

_____   **5.** told the author that he was in Pennsylvania

a. a man digging potatoes

b. an elderly widow

c. James Pennington

d. W. W., a Quaker

e. a young man with a load of hay

Beat! Beat! Drums!

Directions Write *True* if the statement is true; write *False* if it is not true. If the
statement is false, correct it by writing the true fact on the line
provided below that statement.

_____ **1.** Another good title for this poem might be "A Call to War."

_____

_____ **2.** This poem is written in a regular rhythm and rhyme.

_____

_____ **3.** This poem is about recruiting men to serve in the armed forces during war.

_____

_____ **4.** The first line of each stanza repeats the title.

_____

_____ **5.** This poem implies that Walt Whitman was a patriotic American.

_____

_____ **6.** This poem is a very happy one.

_____

_____ **7.** Several important characters are developed in this poem.

_____

_____ **8.** The sounds of the drums and bugles get louder and louder in the poem.

_____

_____ **9.** The poem states that people from a few specific walks of life will
be affected by war.

_____

_____ **10.** Men must go to war even though their families do not want them to go.

_____

Come Up from the Fields Father

Part A Directions   Match the item or person in Column A with its description in Column B. Write the letter of the correct description on the line provided.

Column A

_____ **1.** sky

_____ **2.** apples

_____ **3.** farm

_____ **4.** Pete

_____ **5.** mother

_____ **6.** oldest daughter

_____ **7.** letter

_____ **8.** Ohio

_____ **9.** younger sisters

Column B

a. prosperous, vital

b. teeming and wealthy

c. brave and simple

d. calm, transparent

e. sobbing

f. ripe

g. speechless and dismayed

h. written in a strange hand

i. weeping, faint

Part B Directions   The events in this poem could also be told in prose. Briefly, rewrite the story told in the poem "Come Up from the Fields Father." Use the lines provided below. Use complete sentences.

10. _____

_____

_____

_____

_____

_____

_____

_____

American Literature

A Letter to Mrs. Bixby

Part A Directions Write *True* if the statement is true; write *False* if it is not true. Write your answers on the lines provided.

_____ 1. Mrs. Bixby had four sons.

_____ 2. President Abraham Lincoln asked the Adjutant-General of Massachusetts to write this letter to Mrs. Bixby.

_____ 3. The Adjutant-General of Massachusetts put a statement in the war files about Mrs. Bixby's sons.

_____ 4. President Abraham Lincoln wrote the letter to Mrs. Bixby after the war was over.

_____ 5. These sons all died during the Civil War.

_____ 6. Mrs. Bixby lived in Washington, D.C.

_____ 7. President Abraham Lincoln offered to award a medal of honor for the bravery of Mrs. Bixby's sons.

_____ 8. This letter was written to tell Mrs. Bixby that her sons had died.

_____ 9. President Abraham Lincoln made arrangements to visit Mrs. Bixby in this letter.

_____ 10. President Abraham Lincoln offered his condolences to Mrs. Bixby in this letter.

Part B Directions Read "A Letter to Mrs. Bixby." Then, read each of the following five words that were used in this selection. Read the three meanings listed for each word. Choose the best meaning in each case. Circle your answers.

1. beguile	deceive	smile	grieve
2. consolation	mourning	death	comfort
3. assuage	encounter	increase	lessen
4. anguish	happiness	love	intense sorrow
5. cherished	loved	forgot	saw as unimportant

A Letter to Mrs. Bixby, continued

Part C Directions   Read the following sentences. Choose the sentence that uses the underlined word correctly. Write the letter of your answer on the line provided in each case.

_____ 1. **a.** I want to be a <u>consolation</u>.

              b. It is a <u>consolation</u> to know that he died a hero.

_____ 2. **a.** I will <u>assuage</u> the man at the office.

              b. I will try to <u>assuage</u> your guilt.

_____ 3. **a.** She <u>cherished</u> the antique watch.

              b. I <u>cherished</u> the afternoon bus.

_____ 4. **a.** He <u>sacrificed</u> so that she could go to college.

              b. I <u>sacrificed</u> my homework.

_____ 5. **a.** I felt <u>anguish</u> when my grandparents died.

              b. I felt <u>anguish</u> when I won the award.

_____ 6. **a.** I would not attempt to <u>beguile</u> you in this matter.

              b. I <u>beguile</u> the newspaper every Sunday.

Part D Directions   After each number below there are three words. Circle the words that describe feelings. For each number, there may be one, more than one, or no correct answer.

1. disinterested   anguish   vacant

2. consolation   grief   dreamy

3. exhilaration   counterfeit   seldom

4. bereavement   thrilled   apathetic

What the Black Man Wants

Part A Directions   Match the words with their definitions. Write your answers on the lines provided.

_____ **1.** deprive

_____ **2.** franchise or suffrage

_____ **3.** benevolent

_____ **4.** stigma

_____ **5.** inferior

_____ **6.** sympathy

_____ **7.** incentive

a. a sharing of the feelings of another

b. kind, marked by goodwill

c. the right to vote

d. something that excites someone into action

e. lower status; of less importance

f. mark of shame

g. take away from

Part B Directions   Choose the letter of the answer that best completes each statement about "What the Black Man Wants." Write the letter of your answer on the line provided before each statement.

_____ **1.** "What the Black Man Wants" is an example of a _____.
   a. poem   **b.** speech   **c.** play   **d.** novel

_____ **2.** Frederick Douglass was a former _____.
   a. slave   **b.** minister   **c.** governor   **d.** none of the above

_____ **3.** The author was addressing _____.
   a. the Massachusetts Anti-Slavery Society   **b.** the President Society
   c. a graduating class   **d.** Congress

_____ **4.** Frederick Douglass states that the black man of 1865 wanted _____.
   a. the right to vote   **b.** justice   **c.** to be left alone   **d.** all of the above

_____ **5.** Frederick Douglass uses the apple tree as a symbol for _____.
   a. America   **b.** slavery   **c.** the right to vote   **d.** abolitionists

_____ **6.** The author says that all humans will be better if _____.
   a. nothing is expected of them   **b.** they never vote
   c. some men are treated as inferiors   **d.** none of the above

_____ **7.** The author asks that the African American _____.
   a. have his hands untied   **b.** be left alone
   c. live or die as equals   **d.** all of the above

_____ **8.** The last comment by the author ("I think he will live . . . .") is _____.
   a. a positive one   **b.** unrelated to other sentences
   c. a negative one   **d.** an untrue statement

Life on the Mississippi

Part A Directions   Match the word from Column A with its proper description from Column B. Write the letter of the answer on the line provided.

Column A

Column B

_____ 1. Mississippi	**a.** grandest position of all
_____ 2. pilot	**b.** St. Louis to Keokuk
_____ 3. father	**c.** drunkard, clerks, boys, men
_____ 4. steamboat route	**d.** majestic, magnificent
_____ 5. steamboat	**e.** justice of the peace
_____ 6. townspeople	**f.** sharp, pretty
_____ 7. circus clown	**g.** the boys' transient ambition
_____ 8. clerks	**h.** the boys' permanent ambition
_____ 9. drayman	**i.** sitting on splint-bottomed chairs
_____ 10. steamboatmen	**j.** loafing on the sidewalk
_____ 11. levee	**k.** envied by all the boys
_____ 12. apprentice engineer	**l.** first to notice the arrival of the steamboat
_____ 13. pigs	**m.** landing place for boats on a river
_____ 14. minister's son	**n.** became a mud clerk
_____ 15. postmaster's son	**o.** became an engineer

Part B Directions   Read the following statements describing *Life on the Mississippi*. Decide whether each sentence below represents *Plot, Character, Setting,* or *Point of View*. Write your answer on the line provided.

_____   **1.** The town came alive when the steamboat arrived.

_____   **2.** The boy's father was the justice of the peace.

_____   **3.** I was left in obscurity and misery.

_____   **4.** The streets were empty or nearly so.

_____   **5.** The majestic, magnificent Mississippi rolled by the town.

_____   **6.** The fragrant town drunkard was asleep by the skids on the wharf.

_____   **7.** The boat was a handsome sight with black smoke rolling from the chimneys.

_____   **8.** One boy ran away to become a striker on a steamboat.

_____   **9.** The boys admired and hated this cub engineer.

_____   **10.** I can picture that old town.

The Old Chisholm Trail

Part A Directions   From the words in the Word Bank, choose the word that correctly
completes each statement about "The Old Chisholm Trail." Write the
answers on the lines. Note that some words will not be used.

Word Bank

began
chasing
punchin'
hoss
cow
bacon
troubles
commenced
slicker
outfit
topcoat
biscuits

1. "Rope in my hand and a _____ by the tail."

2. "I'll sell my _____ as soon as I can."

3. "It's _____ and beans most every day."

4. "I'll tell you of my _____ on the old Chisholm trail."

5. "And I'm goin' to _____ Texas cattle."

6. "My _____ throwed me off at the creek called Mud."

7. "The wind _____ to blow, and the rain began to fall . . ."

8. "My _____'s in the wagon and I'm gittin' mighty cold."

Part B Directions   Answer the following questions about the events in the life of a cowhand.
Write your answers in complete sentences on the lines provided.

1. What time did the cowhands get up in the morning?

   _____

2. What weather does the cowhand describe in this song?

   _____

3. How long does the cowhand ride in a day?

   _____

4. What food do the cowhands eat for dinner most days?

   _____

5. What three things does a cowhand carry?

   _____

6. What does a cowhand call his pay?

   _____

7. What is one type of cattle found in the Southwest?

   _____

This Sacred Soil

Part A Directions Write *True* if the statement is true; write *False* if it is not true. Write your answers on the lines provided.

_____ **1.** Seattle was very rude to the white people in his speech.

_____ **2.** Chief Seattle's people, the Duwamish, depended on buffalo for food.

_____ **3.** Seattle felt that the White Man would improve the land greatly.

_____ **4.** Seattle believed that the soil responded better to his people than to the White Men.

_____ **5.** Seattle never referred to the children of his tribe.

_____ **6.** Seattle believed in returning spirits.

_____ **7.** Seattle believed that death was final.

_____ **8.** This land was ceded to the white settlers in 1885.

_____ **9.** "This Sacred Soil" was a speech made by the Governor of Washington.

_____ **10.** Seattle would probably be concerned with environmental issues if he were alive today.

Part B Directions "This Sacred Soil" contains a number of contrasts. Match the words in Column A with contrasting or opposite words in Column B. Write the letters of your answers on the lines provided.

Column A

_____ **1.** happy

_____ **2.** children

_____ **3.** Duwamish and Suquamish

_____ **4.** few people

_____ **5.** hillside

Column B

a. ancestors

b. throngs

c. sad

d. valley

e. settlers

Zuni and Makah Lullabies

Part A Directions   Identify the song from which the following words were taken. Write either "Lullaby" or "My Son" on the lines provided.

1. beetle   _____

2. canoe   _____

3. harpoon   _____

4. jackrabbit   _____

Part B Directions   The Zuni and Makah were very different in many ways. Compare and contrast these two groups of American Indians. Complete the following chart. Write your answers in the spaces provided.

	Zuni	Makah
1. Name of larger group to which they belonged		
2. Geographic area of United States		
3. Description of area		
4. Description of homes		
5. Original occupations		
6. Examples of some present-day occupations		

Unit 3 Review

Directions Look at the sections marked on the map below. Connect each of the following literary selections with the geographic location that is related to that work. Write the letters of the correct locations on the chart at the bottom of this page. Note that three literary selections will have more than one geographic location. Complete the chart by adding the last name of the author and the genre for each work.

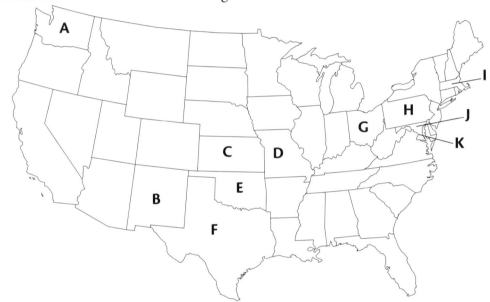

Title	Map Location	Author	Genre
1. *The Fugitive Blacksmith*	(2)		
2. "Thirty-Five"			
3. "Come Up from the Fields Father"			
4. "A Letter to Mrs. Bixby"	(2)		
5. "What the Black Man Wants"			
6. *Life on the Mississippi*			
7. "The Old Chisholm Trail"	(3)		
8. "This Sacred Soil"			
9. "Lullaby"			
10. "My Son"			

Historical Background

Part A Directions Read the words and statements listed below. Choose the correct word from the Word Bank to complete each statement. You will not use all of the words. Write your answer on the line provided in each statement.

Word Bank					
literary	naturalist	nature	literature	newspaper	control
low	countries	romantic	struggle	inner	difficulty

1. Stephen Crane and Jack London fit into the realist and _____ literary movements.

2. Much of the _____ of the time reflected unhappy events.

3. The writing of this period was very different from earlier _____ works.

4. People came to the United States from other _____ seeking new opportunities.

5. Book and _____ publishing was very successful.

6. Characters in Jack London's writings face a force they cannot _____.

7. Many people earned very _____ pay at difficult factory jobs.

8. People faced the reality that life was a _____.

9. Writing of this time included characters who were helpless to understand _____.

10. Stephen Crane examines the _____ nature of humans.

Part B Directions Review the timeline for Unit 4. Identify the year in which each of the following events occurred. Write the correct dates on the lines provided.

_____ 1. The battle of Wounded Knee marks the last of the major Indian wars.

_____ 2. Stephen Crane becomes a newspaper reporter in New York.

_____ 3. Hawaiian Islands are made an American territory.

_____ 4. Stephen Crane publishes "The Open Boat."

_____ 5. Orville and Wilbur Wright fly the first heavier-than-air plane.

_____ 6. The Spanish-American War begins.

_____ 7. Henry Ford introduces the Model T.

_____ 8. Jack London's first novel is published.

_____ 9. The U.S. census shows that about 76 million people live in the United States.

_____ 10. Jack London's "To Build a Fire" is published.

American Literature

The Open Boat

Part A Directions   Write the answer for each of the following questions.
Use complete sentences.

1. What happens in the middle part of the story to make the men believe they will soon be rescued? How do the men react to this?

_____

_____

_____

2. How do the men react when it appears that they will not be helped by these people on land?

_____

_____

_____

_____

3. In Part VII, how does the author show that nature is indifferent to the plight of man?

_____

_____

_____

_____

4. At the end of the story, how does the author show that man can be kind and helpful to man?

_____

_____

_____

5. Describe the overall condition of the men during the time that they were in the dinghy.

_____

_____

_____

The Open Boat, continued

Part B Directions   Listed below are some quotations taken from the short story "The Open Boat." Review your knowledge of literary terms. Decide which of these words best fits each quotation: *Character, Emotion, Action,* or *Nature.* Write your answer on the line provided before each quotation.

_____   **1.** "... waves that seemed thrust up in points like rocks."

_____   **2.** "... the weary-faced oiler smiled in full sympathy."

_____   **3.** "They rowed and they rowed."

_____   **4.** "... there was a great deal of rage in them."

_____   **5.** "'Billie,' he murmured dreamfully, 'what kind of pie do you like best?'"

_____   **6.** "... it merely occurred to him that if he should drown it would be a shame."

_____   **7.** "... the cook bailed it out."

_____   **8.** "A large wave caught him and flung him with ease and supreme speed."

_____   **9.** "... at the mercy of the five oceans."

Part C Directions   "The Open Boat" includes many details about the thoughts of the correspondent after the shipwreck. Choose one of the other characters in the story—the cook, captain, or oiler—and consider the facts given about this character. What do you think this character might have thought about during the many hours at sea in the dinghy? Write your answer on the lines provided below. Use complete sentences.

Character: _____

_____

_____

_____

_____

To Build a Fire

Part A Directions   Match each item in Column A with the correct phrase in Column B.
Write the letter of your answer on the line provided.

Column A

_____ **1.** imperceptible

_____ **2.** depressed

_____ **3.** monotonously

_____ **4.** abruptly

_____ **5.** subdue

_____ **6.** flounder

_____ **7.** temperamental

_____ **8.** devise

_____ **9.** apprehension

_____ **10.** crypt

_____ **11.** intervene

_____ **12.** gait

_____ **13.** reiterate

_____ **14.** unwonted

_____ **15.** compel

Column B

a. without warning

b. to struggle or fail to get proper footing

c. to invent

d. to state or do over again

e. something deep inside

f. to drive or urge forcefully

g. to conquer or bring under control

h. a manner of walking

i. of or relating to how one behaves

j. fear

k. saddened

l. not able to be sensed

m. varying very little

n. unusual

o. to come between

To Build a Fire, continued

Part B Directions   The story "To Build a Fire" is rich with colorful language. Look at each of the words below. After each word, write a passage from the story in which that word appears.

1. trail _____

_____

_____

_____

2. biscuits _____

_____

_____

_____

3. dog _____

_____

_____

_____

4. beard _____

_____

_____

_____

5. creek _____

_____

_____

_____

Unit 4 Review

Part A Directions   Read the Historical Background and the timeline for Unit 4. Which of the
following statements are true of the period of time covered in Unit 4?
Write *True* or *False* on the line before each statement.

_____ 1. The United States was in the middle of the Civil War.

_____ 2. Industry grew in the United States during this time period.

_____ 3. Settlement of the West was taking place.

_____ 4. The new literary movement was called romanticism.

_____ 5. Many people who came to the United States from other countries found
work in factories.

_____ 6. Sermons and diary entries were the most prominent forms of literature.

_____ 7. The first television was invented during this time.

_____ 8. Stephen Crane's characters are victims of cold and grim fate.

_____ 9. Jack London often wrote about characters struggling against nature.

_____ 10. Stephen Crane became a newspaper reporter in New York.

Part B Directions   Write a short paragraph explaining realism and naturalism as literary
movements. List subjects frequently portrayed in realistic and naturalistic
works. Indicate the themes that the two short stories by Crane and London
have in common. Write your paragraph on the lines provided.

_____

_____

_____

_____

_____

_____

Historical Background

Directions Write *True* if the statement is true; write *False* if the statement is not true. Write your answer on the line provided before each statement. Then, if the statement is false, correct it by writing the true fact on the line provided beneath that statement.

_____ **1.** Unit 5: American Literature Comes of Age deals with the nineteenth century.

_____

_____ **2.** The early years of the period were quiet and uneventful.

_____

_____ **3.** The first major event of the century was the Civil War.

_____

_____ **4.** The decade of the twenties was a time of protest and social unrest.

_____

_____ **5.** Radios and airplanes were developed during these years.

_____

_____ **6.** In the year 1929, a stock market crash brought poverty and despair.

_____

_____ **7.** The 1930s were years of unemployment and homelessness for many people.

_____

_____ **8.** American writers tried to avoid issues of the real world in their literature.

_____

_____ **9.** Very few good writers emerged during the early twentieth century.

_____

_____ **10.** Modernism was a literary trend that included many works that were similar to nineteenth century writing.

_____

The Far and the Near

Part A Directions   Read the following phrases taken from the short story "The Far and the Near." Then, choose the letter of the word or words closest in meaning to each of the underlined words. Write the letter of your answer on the line provided before each phrase.

_____ 1. "...a tidy little cottage trimmed <u>vividly</u> with green blinds."
      a. colorfully   **b.** shabbily
      c. quaintly   **d.** oddly

_____ 2. "...he had seen before him on the tracks the <u>ghastly</u> dot of tragedy."
      a. grisly and horrible   **b.** terrible
      c. gruesome   **d.** all of the above

_____ 3. "...something beautiful and <u>enduring</u>..."
      a. lovely   **b.** tender
      c. gently   **d.** long lasting

_____ 4. "...the man <u>plodded</u> on..."
      a. talked endlessly   **b.** laughed
      c. walked slowly   **d.** hurried

_____ 5. "...her face was <u>harsh</u>."
      a. disagreeable   **b.** calm
      c. friendly   **d.** flushed

_____ 6. "...<u>stammering</u> a crude farewell..."
      a. cursing   **b.** yelling
      c. speaking haltingly **d.** speaking quickly

_____ 7. "And finally he <u>departed</u>..."
      a. left   **b.** came in
      c. smiled   **d.** sat down

_____ 8. "...the man sat in an ugly little <u>parlor</u>..."
      a. kitchen   **b.** sitting room
      c. porch   **d.** guest room

_____ 9. "...why did his hand <u>falter</u> on the gate..."
      a. grasp   **b.** hesitate
      c. open   **d.** close

_____ 10. ."...into the <u>drowsy</u> stillness of the afternoon."
      a. sleepy   **b.** calm
      c. quiet   **d.** all of the above

The Far and the Near, continued

Part B Directions   When each event in a story takes place is important to the reader's understanding of the plot. Read the following list of events from "The Far and the Near." Decide on the order in which these events took place. The letter of the first event has been listed for you. On the lines provided, write the letter of the second event after 2, the letter of the third event after 3, etc.

1. __b__

2. _____

3. _____

4. _____

5. _____

6. _____

7. _____

8. _____

9. _____

10. _____

a. The engineer finally meets the woman who lives in the house.

b. The mother and small child wave to the engineer each day.

c. The engineer pauses at the gate of the house.

d. The engineer walks through the town he had so often passed in the train.

e. The engineer retires.

f. The engineer sits with the woman and her daughter in their parlor.

g. The woman invites the engineer inside.

h. The engineer feels old and disappointed.

i. The mother and grown child wave to the engineer.

j. The man walks toward the lordly oaks.

Part C Directions   The following pyramid of dramatic structure shows the plot structure of a short story. "The Far and the Near" can be divided into five parts: *Introduction, Rising Action, Climax, Falling Action,* and *Conclusion.* Write the letter of each event listed in Part B to complete the pyramid below. Some parts will include more than one event.

3. Climax _____

_____

2. Rising Action _____   **4.** Falling Action _____

_____   _____

1. Introduction _____   **5.** Conclusion _____

_____   _____

PLOT STRUCTURE

Theme for English B

Part A Directions   Langston Hughes tells the reader many facts about the narrator in the poem "Theme for English B." He also includes some thoughts that the narrator has. Listed below are several quotations from this poem. Write *Fact* if the statement contains personal data. Write *Opinion* if the statement represents a belief that the narrator has. Write your answer on the line provided.

_____   **1.** "I am twenty-two, colored, . . ."

_____   **2.** "I guess you learn from me . . ."

_____   **3.** "I like to eat, sleep, drink, . . ."

_____   **4.** "I like a pipe for a Christmas present . . ."

_____   **5.** "I guess being colored doesn't make me not like the same things other folks like . . ."

_____   **6.** "Sometimes perhaps you don't want to be a part of me."

_____   **7.** "I am the only colored student in my class."

_____   **8.** ". . . born in Winston-Salem."

_____   **9.** "I wonder if it's that simple?"

_____   **10.** "I went to school there . . ."

Part B Directions   Answer the following questions about "Theme for English B." Write your answers on the lines provided.

1. Read the first stanza. Where did the narrator live before moving to New York?

_____

2. Read the second stanza. List six things Langston Hughes mentions that he likes.

_____

3. Do you share a liking for any of the items mentioned in this second stanza? Explain your answer.

_____

4. In the second stanza, what does the narrator assume about the reader?

_____

5. What primary point does the narrator make in the last stanza?

_____

The Sculptor's Funeral

Part A Directions   Complete the chart below. Add the correct information about "The Sculptor's Funeral."

1. Name of Work/Author	
2. Genre/When and Where Published	
3. Main Character	
4. Supporting Characters	
5. Setting/Plot	
6. Climax	

Part B Directions   Answer the following questions about "The Sculptor's Funeral."

1. Tell whether you like this story or not.

_____

2. Give reasons for your opinion about this story.

_____

_____

3. Which character in this story do you feel sorry for?

_____

_____

4. Explain why you feel sorry for the character.

_____

_____

The Sculptor's Funeral, continued

Part C Directions   Read the names of the characters listed in the Word Bank. Then read the quotations taken from "The Sculptor's Funeral." Identify the speaker of each comment or thought. Write your answer on the line provided in each case. Not all names will be used; some names will be used more than once.

_____ 1. "None of Mr. Merrick's brothers are here?"

_____ 2. "My boy, my boy! And this is how you've come home to me!"

_____ 3. ". . . you mustn't go on like this! . . . The parlor is ready, Mr. Phelps."

_____ 4. "You go on—it'll be a good experience for you. I'm not equal to that crowd tonight; I've had twenty years of them."

| **Word Bank** |
| Mrs. Merrick |
| Harvey Merrick |
| minister |
| Steavens |
| Harvey's sister |
| Phelps |
| Laird |
| cattleman |

_____ 5. "Was it possible that these men did not understand, that the palm on the coffin meant nothing to them?"

_____ 6. ". . . after they have had their say, I shan't have much to fear from the judgment of God!"

_____ 7. "Forty's young for a Merrick to cash in . . . Probably he helped it along with whiskey."

_____ 8. ". . . Harvey never had a robust constitution."

_____ 9. ". . . we wanted you all to be proud of us someday. We meant to be great men."

_____ 10. "Harvey Merrick wouldn't have given one sunset over your marshes for all you've got put together, and you know it . . . ."

The Freshest Boy

Part A Directions   Read the following questions about "The Freshest Boy." Choose the correct answer in each case. Write the letter of the correct answer on the line provided before each question.

_____ **1.** What is the name of the school that Basil attends?
      a. St. Regis   **b.** St. Paul's
      c. School #32   **d.** Eastchester

_____ **2.** Who is the headmaster of this school?
      a. Doctor Smythe   **b.** Doctor David
      c. Doctor Bacon   **d.** Mr. Wales

_____ **3.** Basil applied for permission to go into what city?
      a. New York   **b.** Westchester
      c. Eastchester   **d.** Los Angeles

_____ **4.** How did the headmaster describe Basil's grades?
      a. excellent   **b.** poor
      c. failing   **d.** improving nicely

_____ **5.** How is Basil viewed by the other boys?
      a. very popular   **b.** everybody's friend
      c. quite well liked   **d.** unpopular

_____ **6.** What is the eventual career of Bugs Brown?
      a. convict   **b.** famous doctor
      c. headmaster   **d.** brilliant lawyer

_____ **7.** Where did Basil locate Fat Gaspar to invite him to the trip?
      a. Ice Cream Shoppe   **b.** grocery store
      c. Bostonian Candy Kitchen   **d.** library

_____ **8.** Where does Basil's grandfather want to take Basil and his mother?
      a. Florida   **b.** abroad
      c. California   **d.** the Midwest

_____ **9.** Whom did Basil see in the lobby of the theater?
      a. the Yale football captain   **b.** the headmaster of his school
      c. a famous actress   **d.** his mother

_____ **10.** Basil finally felt that he was making friends when he was called a nickname while playing what sport?
      a. soccer   **b.** polo
      c. football   **d.** basketball

The Freshest Boy, continued

Part B Directions   Identify the word that is nearest to the meaning of the underlined word in each sentence below. Write the letter of the correct answer on the line provided.

_____ 1. He traversed a long corridor.
   a. walked across   b. looked across
   c. avoided   d. stumbled down

_____ 2. He shuffled through the papers.
   a. read carefully   b. leafed
   c. walked   d. made noise with

_____ 3. They have purchased seats together.
   a. attached   b. bought
   c. selected   d. taken without permission

_____ 4. What made him the most detested boy in school?
   a. admired   b. envied
   c. hated   d. popular

_____ 5. They held him and dressed him down savagely.
   a. complained about him   b. yelled at
   c. laughed at his clothes d. ignored him

_____ 6. Puzzled and wretched, he looked at his face in the glass.
   a. miserable   b. sincere
   c. scary   d. stretched

_____ 7. He had become the sponge which absorbed all malice.
   a. fear   b. dirt
   c. envy   d. hatred

_____ 8. Boys taunted him.
   a. beat   b. enjoyed
   c. insulted   d. envied

_____ 9. Then he dashed around a corner.
   a. crawled   b. walked slowly
   c. hopped   d. hurried

_____ 10. This is written in great haste.
   a. happiness   b. speed
   c. care   d. ease

The Freshest Boy, continued

Part C Directions   Read the names of the characters listed in the Word Bank. Then, read the quotations taken from "The Freshest Boy." Identify the character associated with the quote in each case. Write your answer on the line provided before each quotation. Not all names will be used; some names will be used more than once.

_____   1.   "He was a handsome, redheaded clergyman of fifty whose original real interest in boys was now tempered by the flustered cynicism . . ."

_____   2.   "He knew that he was one of the poorest boys in a rich boys' school."

_____   3.   "I don't want to go," he said indifferently. "Why do you want to ask me?"

_____   4.   ". . . a crowd of the smaller boys . . . gathered suddenly around him and began calling him Bossy."

_____   5.   ". . . a hysterical boy, subject to fits and strenuously avoided."

_____   6.   "He was considered a nice fellow—in fact he was so pleasant that he had been courteous to Basil and had spoken politely to him all fall."

_____   7.   ". . . had entered St. Regis late in the year and had been put in to room with Basil the week before."

_____   8.   "a boy [Basil] had had a fight with and one of his bitterest enemies."

_____   9.   ". . . in fact he was a hard specimen and Doctor Bacon was planning to get rid of him at Christmas."

_____   10.   ". . . you didn't have any nerve. You could play better than a lot of 'em when you wanted . . . but you lost your nerve."

_____   11.   "I've got some business of my own I got to attend to, and when I've finished I'll try to get to the show."

_____   12.   "This is written in great haste . . . [I] will be leaving home almost as soon as you get this and will come to the Waldorf in New York . . ."

_____   13.   ". . . the Yale football captain, who had almost single-handed beaten Harvard and Princeton last fall."

_____   14.   "a radiant little beauty of nineteen . . ."

_____   15.   "I'm living up to my responsibility to Beltzman."

Word Bank

Basil Lee
Ted Fay
Doctor Bacon
Fat Gaspar
Mr. Rooney
Treadway
Bugs Brown
Brick Wales
Carver
Fay's woman
   friend
Basil's mother

Mending Wall

Directions Write *True* if the statement is true; write *False* if the statement is not true. Write your answer on the line provided before each statement. Then, if the statement is false, correct it by writing the true fact on the line provided below the statement.

_____ **1.** The title of the poem has nothing to do with the subject of the poem.

_____

_____ **2.** Some hunters have made gaps in the wall.

_____

_____ **3.** The narrator has peach trees.

_____

_____ **4.** Each spring the two neighbors fix the wall.

_____

_____ **5.** The wall is made of bricks.

_____

_____ **6.** The two neighbors share their crops and fields.

_____

_____ **7.** The author believes that walls should surround one's land.

_____

_____ **8.** The author questions the opinion "Good fences make good neighbors."

_____

_____ **9.** The wall successfully keeps dogs and hunters off the property.

_____

_____ **10.** I agree with the neighbor "that good fences make good neighbors."

_____

A Time to Talk and Fire and Ice

Part A Directions Certain words used in the poem "A Time to Talk" convey the picture of a scene for the reader. Listed below are several words that could further describe this scene. Write *Yes* before those words that match the scene described in "A Time to Talk." Write *No* before those words that do not describe the scene in this poem.

_____ **1.** lake

_____ **2.** rich earth

_____ **3.** apple pie

_____ **4.** dusty lane

_____ **5.** hot sun

_____ **6.** tractor

_____ **7.** late phone call

_____ **8.** hearty wave

Part B Directions Read the words listed in the Word Bank. Choose the correct word to complete each statement about "Fire and Ice." Note that some words will not be used. Write your answers on the lines provided.

Word Bank				
hate	plot	tone	desire	rhyme
dialect	stanza	contrasts	end	

1. "Fire and Ice," as its title suggests, is a poem of _____.

2. The poet says he has tasted _____.

3. The poet says that the world will certainly _____ once, perhaps twice.

4. The _____ of this poem is grave and grim.

5. The poet says that he knows enough of _____.

6. This poem has only one _____.

7. Unlike some of Robert Frost's poems, "Fire and Ice" does contain _____.

Impulse

Part A Directions   Complete the chart below. Add the correct information about "Impulse."

1. Name of work/Author	
2. Genre	
3. Main character	
4. Supporting characters	
5. Setting: Places	
6. Setting: Time	
7. Plot	
8. Turning point or climax	

Part B Directions   Answer the following questions about "Impulse."

1. What is your opinion of the main character?

   _____

   _____

2. Give reasons for your opinion.

   _____

   _____

   _____

Impulse, continued

Part C Directions   Read the following sentences about the short story "Impulse." Choose the definition that is closest in meaning to each underlined word. Write the letter of the correct answer on the line provided before each statement.

_____ **1.** Michael and Dora had a <u>row</u> about unpaid bills.
    a. discussion   **b.** fight
    c. laugh   **d.** fear

_____ **2.** Dora was quiet but not <u>hostile</u> at breakfast.
    a. pitiful   **b.** funny
    c. angry   **d.** sad

_____ **3.** He developed the idea with <u>gusto</u>.
    a. common sense   **b.** humor
    c. no real interest   **d.** enthusiasm

_____ **4.** An impulse could be described as a universal human <u>inclination</u>.
    a. tendency   **b.** complaint
    c. look   **d.** joke

_____ **5.** He would <u>simultaneously</u> close it and remove it.
    a. carefully   **b.** quickly
    c. slowly   **d.** occurring at the same time

_____ **6.** The detective managed to convey <u>venom</u> in his words to Michael.
    a. poisonous ill will   **b.** delight
    c. fear   **d.** affection

_____ **7.** Dora had lived with the humiliation of <u>duns</u>.
    a. demands for bill payment   **b.** shoplifting
    c. crimes   **d.** poverty

_____ **8.** Here was a perfectly clear case of theft and a clear <u>motive</u>.
    a. excuse   **b.** explanation
    c. reason for acting   **d.** cause

_____ **9.** After his trial, Michael was in a state of complete <u>stupor</u>.
    a. happiness   **b.** anger
    c. excitement   **d.** shock

_____ **10.** Dora hoped Michael would refrain from <u>contesting</u> the divorce.
    a. wishing for   **b.** challenging
    c. agreeing to   **d.** bringing about

Jazz Fantasia

Part A Directions Match each instrument in the first column with the word associated with that instrument in the second column. Write the letter of the correct answer on the line provided.

_____ **1.** banjos   **a.** sob

_____ **2.** saxophones   **b.** bang

_____ **3.** trombones   **c.** ooze

_____ **4.** drums   **d.** happy

_____ **5.** sandpaper   **e.** slippery

_____ **6.** tin pans   **f.** batter

Part B Directions Answer the following questions by circling the correct answer below the question.

1. Who wrote "Jazz Fantasia"?

Carl Sandburg   Langston Hughes   Robert Frost

2. How many stanzas does this poem have?

one   four   five

3. Does this poem contain rhyme?

no   in places   yes

4. The author of "Jazz Fantasia" is also noted as the famous biographer of what president?

George Washington   Theodore Roosevelt   Abraham Lincoln

5. This poem uses what literary device to imitate certain sounds?

alliteration   onomatopoeia   assonance

6. What mood is expressed by the music in this poem?

excitement   fear   sadness

7. What refrain is repeated several times in this poem?

"Go husha-hush"   "Go to it, O jazzmen"   "Drum on your drums"

8. Based on your reading of this poem, what subject do you believe the author knows very well?

weather   music   noise

9. Of what pleasant image does the music remind the author?

two people fighting   the Mississippi at night   the Paris Opera

Cool Tombs

Directions Write *True* if the statement is true; write *False* if the statement is not true. Write your answer on the line provided before each statement. Then, if the answer is false, correct it by writing the true fact on the line provided below that statement.

_____ **1.** Carl Sandburg uses a certain refrain in "Cool Tombs."

_____

_____ **2.** This poem contains seven stanzas.

_____

_____ **3.** This poem is an example of free verse.

_____

_____ **4.** Cool Tombs" is a poem about hate.

_____

_____ **5.** In this poem, Sandburg mentions great men and women who are still alive.

_____

_____ **6.** The author tells of common people buying clothes and groceries.

_____

_____ **7.** He also says that common people sometimes cheer a hero and throw dice.

_____

_____ **8.** This poem uses the word *grave* many times.

_____

_____ **9.** This poem suggests that everyone will eventually lie in cool tombs.

_____

_____ **10.** The last stanza of the poem tells us that Abraham Lincoln was assassinated.

_____

Unit 5 Review

Part A Directions   Reread the Historical Background and the timeline for Unit 5, as well as each Introducing the Selection. Find the correct date for each event described below. Write your answers on the lines provided.

_____   **1.** World War I begins in Europe.

_____   **2.** The United States enters World War I.

_____   **3.** The first television becomes available.

_____   **4.** The first talking motion picture is produced.

_____   **5.** Carl Sandburg receives a Pulitzer Prize for his biography of Abraham Lincoln.

_____   **6.** The stock market crashes.

_____   **7.** Langston Hughes publishes *The Weary Blues.*

_____   **8.** Women receive the right to vote.

_____   **9.** Willa Cather publishes "A Sculptor's Funeral."

_____   **10.** Robert Frost receives a gold medal from Congress for his poetry.

| 1960 |
| 1917 |
| 1905 |
| 1914 |
| 1939 |
| 1920 |
| 1926 |
| 1927 |
| 1940 |
| 1929 |

Part B Directions   Setting describes the place and time in which a story occurs. Each of the works included in this unit takes place in or is associated with a very different location. Match each title with the setting described in that work. Write the letter of your answer on the line provided.

_____   **1.** "The Sculptor's Funeral"

_____   **2.** "Fire and Ice"

_____   **3.** "The Far and the Near"

_____   **4.** "Cool Tombs"

_____   **5.** "Theme for English B"

_____   **6.** "The Freshest Boy"

_____   **7.** "A Time to Talk"

_____   **8.** "Jazz Fantasia"

_____   **9.** "Impulse"

_____   **10.** "Mending Wall"

a. Harlem in New York

b. a road by a farm in New England

c. an expensive boys' boarding school

d. the world of music

e. a cottage, with trees and a garden, in a small town

f. a graveyard or cemetery

g. the parlor of a house in Sand City

h. the boundary line between two neighbors

i. the world

j. an apartment, restaurant, drugstore, police station, jail, and courtroom

Unit 5 Review, continued

Part C Directions   Complete the chart at the bottom of this page. List the title, author, and genre for each work described below. Write your answers in the spaces provided in the chart.

1. A student learns how a dead man's past affected his life.
2. An author discusses the power of love and hate.
3. Two neighbors meet to repair the boundary between their land.
4. A train engineer learns that things are not always what they seem.
5. A student wishes to be accepted by boys at his school.
6. Two neighbors pause for a friendly visit.
7. Sentences capture the mood and sounds of 1920s music.
8. A student describes his neighborhood, his life, and his relationships.
9. The decision to steal ruins a man's life.
10. An author discusses the deaths of both famous and ordinary people.

	TITLE	AUTHOR	GENRE
1.			
2.			
3.			
4.			
5.			
6.			
7.			
8.			
9.			
10.			

Historical Background

Part A Directions   Read the following list of events discussed in the Historical Background to Unit 6. They are actual events of the time, but they are not listed in correct chronological order. Letter the events as they actually occurred during this period. Write the letter of the first event after 1, the letter of the second event after 2, and so on. Write your answers on the lines provided.

1. _____   **a.** The Vietnam War shattered peace and optimism.

2. _____   **b.** The United States became involved in the Korean War.

3. _____   **c.** Americans found a commitment to social causes.

4. _____   **d.** The civil rights movement began.

5. _____   **e.** World War II was finally over.

6. _____   **f.** People did not show much interest in the economy, society, or politics.

7. _____   **g.** Protesting greatly divided the country.

8. _____   **h.** Growth was evident in industry, transportation, communication, and education.

Part B Directions   Circle the best answer to complete each statement below.

1. During this time, the United States became one of the most (powerful, feared, ignored) nations in the world.

2. After World War II ended, a boom in the economy took place as the (lower class, middle class, upper class) grew.

3. (Hospitals, Shelters, Schools) became overcrowded after World War II.

4. During the 1950s, many American people feared the growth of (democratic, communist, foreign) governments.

5. In the mid-1960s, American dreams of peace were shattered by (the Korean War, the Vietnam War, economic problems).

6. During (World War II, the Korean War, the Vietnam War), fifty-five million people were killed.

7. Most of the fighting in World War II took place in (Japan, the United States, Europe).

To Be Young, Gifted and Black

Directions   Listed below are a number of facts told in the first-person point of view; however, not all of them could apply to Lorraine Hansberry's *To Be Young, Gifted and Black*. If the statement is true about Lorraine Hansberry, write *Yes* on the line provided. If the statement is not true about the author, write *No*.

_____   **1.**   I was born in Chicago.

_____   **2.**   I was the oldest child in my family.

_____   **3.**   There were seven children in my family.

_____   **4.**   We were taught that we were better than no one but infinitely superior to everyone.

_____   **5.**   My neighborhood was on the Southside.

_____   **6.**   I came from a wealthy neighborhood.

_____   **7.**   I was born in the eighteenth century.

_____   **8.**   My father died when I was very young.

_____   **9.**   My father was a doctor.

_____   **10.**   I played games with other children outside in the summer.

_____   **11.**   Sometimes families spent the night in the park because it was so hot.

_____   **12.**   My sister and I are very close in age.

_____   **13.**   My father knew many facts about American history.

_____   **14.**   I always felt appreciated by the members of my family and was hugged frequently.

_____   **15.**   I remember the many lovely, expensive clothes that I had as a child.

The Killers

Part A Directions   Choose the best answer from the Word Bank to complete each sentence about "The Killers." Some answers will not be used. Write your answers on the lines.

Word Bank					
Swede	overcoats	six	eggs	friend	sweaters
Chicago	two	ring	Summit	Hirsch's	double-crossed
reward	derby	straw	army	seven	

1. At five o'clock, _____ men came into Henry's lunch-room.

2. Dinner could not be ordered until _____ o'clock.

3. Both men ate _____.

4. The name of the town in which the story takes place is _____.

5. The men wore their _____ while they ate.

6. The men said that they were going to kill a _____ named Andreson.

7. They said that they were killing him for a _____.

8. The men left the lunch-room at five minutes after _____.

9. The men wore _____ hats as they crossed the street.

10. Ole Andreson lived at _____ rooming-house.

11. It was obvious from his face that Ole had once been in the _____.

12. George thought that Ole must have gotten into trouble while in _____.

13. George said that Ole must have _____ somebody.

Name

Date

Period

Unit 6

Workbook

50

page 2

The Killers, continued

Part B Directions   Time is important in "The Killers." The characters are constantly remind-
ing each other and the reader of the time. Some major events of the story
are listed below, but they are out of order. Write the letter of the first event
after 1, the letter of the second event after 2, and so on. Write your answers
on the lines provided.

1. _____   **a.** Max and Al say that they are looking for Ole Andreson.

2. _____   **b.** Max and Al leave the lunch-room.

3. _____   **c.** Nick decides to leave town.

4. _____   **d.** The gangsters force George and Nick to go behind the counter.

5. _____   **e.** Nick decides to go see Ole Andreson and warn him.

6. _____   **f.** The two men order something to eat.

7. _____   **g.** Nick talks to the landlady.

Flight

Part A Directions   Write *True* if the statement is true; write *False* if the statement is not true. Write your answers on the lines provided.

_____   **1.** The setting for this story is a small farm near Monterey, California.

_____   **2.** The Torres family raised racehorses.

_____   **3.** Mama Torres is a large, heavyset woman.

_____   **4.** The father of the Torres family died when he fell from his horse.

_____   **5.** Pepé is the oldest of the Torres children.

_____   **6.** Pepé has black hair and sharp cheekbones.

_____   **7.** Pepé often plays with his gun.

_____   **8.** Pepé is sent into town for shoes and candy.

_____   **9.** Pepé added a hat and handkerchief for the ride into town.

_____   **10.** Pepé planned to stay with the Rodriguez family for the night.

_____   **11.** Emilio was the name of Pepé's horse.

_____   **12.** Mama Torres made tortillas out of corn flour.

_____   **13.** The young Torres children used iron hooks to catch abalones.

_____   **14.** Pepé drank wine while in town.

_____   **15.** Pepé told his mother that he had killed a man who insulted him.

_____   **16.** Pepé looked exactly the same after he returned from the trip.

_____   **17.** Mama gave Pepé a rifle and ten cartridges.

_____   **18.** Mama Torres cried when Pepé left for the second time.

_____   **19.** The little Torres house overlooked a river.

_____   **20.** The other children believed that Pepé would live.

Flight, continued

Part B Directions   Listed below are several settings and sounds that are used in many short stories. Some of these settings and sounds are taken from the story "Flight." Others are not. Write *Yes* if the phrase describes something in "Flight." Write *No* if the phrase does not describe something in this short story. Write your answers on the lines provided.

_____   **1.** the wild Pacific coast

_____   **2.** the Mississippi riverbanks

_____   **3.** a small town in New England

_____   **4.** a large, lovely house

_____   **5.** the sound of the ocean

_____   **6.** a rattling, rotting barn

_____   **7.** a busy city

_____   **8.** stone mountains against the sky

_____   **9.** a little growth of corn from sterile slopes

_____   **10.** lush, lovely green hills

_____   **11.** palm trees and sand

_____   **12.** abundant crops growing in rows

Part C Directions   The following words were used in the story "Flight." Match these words with their definitions. Write the letters of your answers on the lines provided.

_____   **1.** gangling   **a.** mollusks; sea animals with soft bodies and hard shells

_____   **2.** keen   **b.** a stone used for grinding grains, especially corn

_____   **3.** labor   **c.** lanky, thin; awkwardly built

_____   **4.** abalones   **d.** meat preserved in long sun-dried slices

_____   **5.** jerky   **e.** a lament or wail for the dead

_____   **6.** agilely   **f.** a task or job; work

_____   **7.** dulces   **g.** sweets or candy

_____   **8.** metate   **h.** moving with quick and easy grace

American Literature

In Honor of David Anderson Brooks, My Father

Part A Directions   Write the letter of the word or phrase that best completes each statement. Write the correct letter on the line provided before each statement.

_____   1. The author says that her father had "loved and tended" his _____.
   a. children   **b.** garden   **c.** animals   **d.** house

_____   2. The atmosphere in the house is now one of _____.
   a. dryness   **b.** cheer   **c.** gloom   **d.** regret

_____   3. The author believes that her father "replies to _____ forever."
   a. mountains   **b.** a grave   **c.** sun and wind   **d.** hell

_____   4. "My father's soul revives" in the _____.
   a. grave   **b.** cool tombs   **c.** church   **d.** wide clean air

_____   5. The father is described as having been _____.
   a. afraid to die **b.** smart   **c.** mean   **d.** free of self-interest

_____   6. The poet remembers that her father was _____.
   a. a lecturer   **b.** well educated **c.** very moody   **d.** gentle and dignified

_____   7. The poem indicates that the father had _____.
   a. been sick   **b.** died suddenly
   c. had an accident **d.** committed suicide

_____   8. The poet probably wrote this poem _____.
   a. soon after his death   **b.** while in her twenties
   c. for money   **d.** quickly

_____   9. The poem suggests that Mr. Brooks was _____.
   a. loved   **b.** feared   **c.** a difficult man **d.** self-centered

_____   10. The poem also suggests that Mr. Brooks was _____.
   a. a private man **b.** loud and funny **c.** a talented entertainer **d.** demanding

Part B Directions   Complete each quotation by writing the correct words on the lines provided. Choose your answer from the Word Bank. Not all words will be used.

   1. "A dryness is upon the _____"

   2. "He walks the _____, now. . ."

   3. "Now out upon the wide clean _____/
   My father's soul revives,"

   4. "All innocent of _____"

   5. "No more the hindering _____."

> **Word Bank**
> valleys
> fever
> self-interest
> vanity
> air
> house

The Catbird Seat

Directions   Choose the correct answer to complete each sentence about "The Catbird Seat." Circle the correct answer in each case.

1. The main character in this story is (Mr. Hart, Mr. Fitweiler, Mr. Martin, Mr. Manson).

2. This story takes place in (Chicago, Springfield, Seattle, New York).

3. The hero of this story is the head of the (filing, advertising, production, sales) department at F & S.

4. The main character hates the woman named (Mrs. Barrows, Mrs. Fitweiler, Mrs. Payne, Mrs. Straus).

5. The hero especially hated the way this woman (talked, dressed, walked, smoked).

6. The hero daydreams that a (doctor, judge, minister, teacher) is listening to his reasons for hating this woman.

7. "The Catbird Seat" was supposed to have taken place during the (1960s, 1980s, 1940s, 1970s).

8. The main character in this story always drank a glass of (beer, wine, soda, milk) after a day of work.

9. While at the woman's apartment, the hero searches for a (magazine, weapon, coat, report).

10. In the apartment, the main character had a cigarette and a (soda, highball, cup of coffee, glass of wine).

11. He told the woman that he used (marijuana, tranquilizers, heroin, crack).

12. During this visit, the hero told the woman that he was planning to (kill, lie to, befriend, listen to) their boss.

13. The next morning, the main character arrived at the office (on time, around ten o'clock, earlier than usual, a little late).

14. After he heard her story, the boss believed that the annoying woman had (told the truth, quit, taken another job, had a breakdown).

15. The hero in this story was successful in his effort to (get a raise, move away, get married, get the woman fired).

Hiroshima

Directions The selection from *Hiroshima* covers that time right after the explosion of the atomic bomb. The statements below describe things the
Reverend Mr. Tanimoto did after the explosion. After the numbers,
write the letters of the events in the order in which they occurred.

1. _____

2. _____

3. _____

4. _____

5. _____

6. _____

7. _____

8. _____

9. _____

10. _____

11. _____

12. _____

13. _____

14. _____

15. _____

a. He saw that a thick miasma lay over the city.

b. He began to run, in fear, toward the city.

c. Mr. Tanimoto helped an old woman.

d. Huge drops of water fell from the sky.

e. From the mound, he saw a panorama.

f. He took the woman and child to a grammar school used as a hospital.

g. He thought of a hillock in the rayon man's garden.

h. He saw houses nearby burning.

i. He looked wildly out of the Matsui estate.

j. Clumps of smoke pushed up through the dust.

k. Mr. Tanimoto thought that the sky was very silent.

l. He looked at the bloody soldiers at the mouth of the dugout.

m. Mr. Tanimoto thought of his own wife and child.

n. Mr. Matsuo called out, asking whether he was all right.

o. Then he ran back to the estate for a view of Hiroshima.

Notes of a Native Son

Directions   Choose the word or phrase to complete each statement about this selection. Write the letter of the correct answer on the line provided before each statement.

_____   **1.** This selection is an example of _____.
     a. a poem   **b.** a novel   **c.** an essay   **d.** a play

_____   **2.** The author was raised in _____.
     a. Paris   **b.** Washington   **c.** Los Angeles   **d.** Harlem

_____   **3.** The author _____ frequently during his childhood.
     a. read   **b.** wrote   **c.** babysat   **d.** all of the above

_____   **4.** At the age of fourteen, James Baldwin became a _____.
     a. dropout   **b.** preacher   **c.** millionaire   **d.** professor

_____   **5.** The author completed his first novel at the age of _____.
     a. 45   **b.** 60   **c.** 22   **d.** 10

_____   **6.** Later the author moved to _____.
     a. New York   **b.** Paris   **c.** Rome   **d.** Seattle

_____   **7.** The author says the _____ is written about too often and too badly.
     a. Negro problem   **b.** Civil War   **c.** President   **d.** European situation

_____   **8.** According to the author, the business of a writer is to _____.
     a. examine attitudes   **b.** go beneath the surface
     c. tap the source   **d.** all of the above

_____   **9.** James Baldwin realized that his past was traced to _____, not Europe.
     a. South America   **b.** Canada
     c. Switzerland   **d.** Africa

_____   **10.** James Baldwin says that most writers write about _____.
     a. love   **b.** hate
     c. their own experiences   **d.** the world

_____   **11.** The author would like to own a camera so that he can _____.
     a. become famous   **b.** make movies
     c. feel wealthy   **d.** live in Paris

_____   **12.** The author does not like people whose principal aim is _____.
     a. writing   **b.** pleasure   **c.** travel   **d.** literary criticism

_____   **13.** The author says that he does not like people who either like or dislike him simply because he is _____.
     a. Negro   **b.** tall   **c.** living in Europe   **d.** rich

_____   **14.** The author states that he loves _____ more than any other country in the world.
     a. France   **b.** Canada   **c.** Mexico   **d.** America

_____   **15.** The author says that he wants to be a good _____.
     a. provider   **b.** salesman   **c.** preacher   **d.** writer

Stride Toward Freedom: The Montgomery Story

Directions In the selection from *Stride Toward Freedom: The Montgomery Story,* Martin Luther King, Jr., mentions three ways in which people deal with oppression. Each statement below represents one of those ways of dealing with oppression. Write the number of each statement under the correct heading in the chart below.

1. The family hired an attorney to sue the realtor who refused to show them a house in a "white" neighborhood.
2. Martin was used to being called names, so he did nothing about it.
3. The girls decided to start carrying knives to protect themselves from possible abuse.
4. The workers went on strike to protest unsafe working conditions.
5. Charlene didn't mind taking a different bus because she didn't feel like riding with the snobby group of students anyway.
6. Bart didn't return the man's punch, but he asked the man why he found it necessary to punch people who are different.
7. The store owner was known for his racist views, so African Americans stopped shopping in his place of business.
8. The boys always walked to school in groups so that they would be less likely to get harmed.
9. Every time their wall was painted with hateful messages, the Bergrens repainted it.
10. Brian had often frightened little Joey, until Joey's brother James gave Brian a black eye.
11. Mrs. Carter moved her children to an inferior school, but at least there they would not be taunted.
12. The Dogface Gang would do anything to keep people who were unlike them out of their neighborhood.
13. Whenever the first team yelled cruel remarks, the second team yelled cruel remarks right back at them.
14. If you wanted to go to that church, you simply had to sit in the back.
15. When Marion first walked into the room, everyone ignored her, but after the third week people started talking to her.

AQUIESCENCE	VIOLENCE	NONVIOLENT RESISTANCE

Monet's "Waterlilies"

Directions Choose the correct word from the Word Bank to complete each sentence below.

Word Bank			
dissolve	picture	time	poison
news	illusive	shadow	lost
tears	fallout		

1. The author refers to loving a serene great _____.

2. He says that _____ has come today from Vietnam and civil rights protests.

3. These headlines _____ the air.

4. The nuclear particles referred to are called _____.

5. In the "Waterlilies," space and _____ exist in light.

6. Those things both seen and known _____ in iridescence.

7. Those things both seen and known become _____ flesh of light.

8. The light is seen as though through refracting _____.

9. The author says that each of us has _____ the aura of a serene world.

10. In the "Waterlilies," the author sees the _____ of the world's joy.

Unit 6 Review

Part A Directions   Before each statement below, write the letter of the author
or authors described. Many letters will be used more than once.

_____   **1.** Awarded a Nobel Prize

_____   **2.** Was interested in writing about adventure

_____   **3.** Elected to the National Academy of American Poets

_____   **4.** Wrote an award-winning Broadway play

_____   **5.** Received a Pulitzer Prize

_____   **6.** Once worked for a newspaper

_____   **7.** One of the first major writers to use
California as a setting

_____   **8.** Wrote several works in Paris

_____   **9.** Was also a cartoonist

_____   **10.** Wrote much historical fiction

_____   **11.** Was named Poet Laureate of Illinois

_____   **12.** Born in China

_____   **13.** Died before reaching age 40

_____   **14.** Was a preacher

_____   **15.** Was one of greatest humorous writers of all time

a. Lorraine Hansberry
b. Ernest Hemingway
c. John Steinbeck
d. Gwendolyn Brooks
e. James Thurber
f. John Hersey
g. James Baldwin
h. Martin Luther King, Jr.
i. Robert Hayden

Unit 6 Review, continued

Part B Directions Match each item in Column A with the correct phrase in Column B. Write the letters of your answers on the lines provided.

Column A

_____ **1.** landward

_____ **2.** vanity

_____ **3.** affinities

_____ **4.** derby

_____ **5.** utilitarian

_____ **6.** expectant

_____ **7.** pulverize

_____ **8.** peccadillo

_____ **9.** aphid

_____ **10.** hindering

_____ **11.** invariably

_____ **12.** vaudeville

_____ **13.** anticipate

_____ **14.** croquette

_____ **15.** profoundly

Column B

a. practical; useful

b. constantly

c. give advance thought to

d. stage entertainment of singing, dancing, or comedy

e. greatly, deeply

f. great pride in oneself or one's appearance

g. small mass of minced meat or fish breaded and deep fried

h. attractions; sympathetic relationships

i. waiting for something to happen

j. a slight offense

k. toward the land

l. type of felt hat with a dome-shaped crown and a narrow brim

m. to crush; to grind into small pieces

n. hampering, blocking, or slowing progress

o. small insect that sucks juices from plants

Historical Background

Directions   Read the following statements. If the statement is false, rewrite it correctly on the line below the sentence. If the statement is true, write *True* on the line.

1. The past thirty years have been free of many historical events.

_____

2. Richard Nixon resigned as President in 1974.

_____

3. American and United Nations forces freed Iraq from invasion by Kuwait in the Persian Gulf War.

_____

4. The 300th anniversary of our nation was celebrated in 1976.

_____

5. Ronald Reagan immediately followed Richard Nixon as the next U.S. President.

_____

6. Large American cities solved their problems of homelessness and joblessness in the 1980s.

_____

7. The economy reached an all-time high during the 1980s.

_____

8. A woman, Sandra Day O'Connor, was appointed to the Supreme Court in 1981.

_____

9. In recent years, very little ethnic literature has been recognized.

_____

10. Contemporary literature reflects the unique and varied identity of the American people.

_____

A City of Words

Directions Write *True* if the statement is true; write *False* if the statement is not true. Write your answers on the lines provided.

_____ **1.** As Richard Rodriguez learned English, he found he could no longer speak Spanish fluently.

_____ **2.** The author did not feel at all guilty about losing his Spanish fluency.

_____ **3.** Members of his family called him *"Pocho"* because they were so proud of him.

_____ **4.** The author's family came from Spain.

_____ **5.** The story describes meal times at the Rodriguez household.

_____ **6.** The author's parents were often embarrassed about his poor Spanish.

_____ **7.** The author's grandmother was very angry that her grandson had become anglicized.

_____ **8.** Spanish-speaking family friends were sometimes even abusive to Richard because he had lost much of his parents' language.

_____ **9.** The author felt he had shattered the bond between himself and his English-speaking friends.

_____ **10.** The author came to feel more intimate with friends as his English fluency improved.

_____ **11.** The author translated his grandmother's words for his friend.

_____ **12.** The author and his family became more intimate once they all spoke English.

_____ **13.** The author felt that his house was noisier when his family spoke Spanish than when they spoke English.

_____ **14.** Intimate moments, says the author, are usually quiet.

_____ **15.** The author believed that intimacy was always created by language.

Poems by Lucille Clifton

Part A Directions Read Lucille Clifton's two poems. Then identify the poem from which the following words were taken. Write the abbreviation for the correct title on the line before each phrase.

_____ **1.** "making a world"

_____ **2.** "an echo of her life"

_____ **3.** "frowns in the glass"

_____ **4.** "with wood"

_____ **5.** "glint of likeness"

_____ **6.** "only sin was dying"

_____ **7.** "his fingers cut"

_____ **8.** "only a poem"

| (MM) morning mirror |
| (MDP) my dream about the poet |

Part B Directions Based on the two poems that you have read, which of the following words or phrases apply to Lucille Clifton's style of writing? Write *Yes* if the phrase applies to her style of writing; write *No* if it does not apply to her style.

_____ **1.** keen observation

_____ **2.** long narrative verse

_____ **3.** lowercase letters

_____ **4.** short poems

_____ **5.** deep reflection or thought

_____ **6.** rhyming patterns

_____ **7.** themes of hatred

The Starfish

Part A Directions The author uses vivid images to describe the starfish, parts of the starfish, and its movement and positions. Circle the noun in each pair that does *not* appear in the poem as an image.

   1. puppy   flower

   2. snake   carbon paper

   3. fire   glacier

   4. skyscraper   dinosaur

   5. horse   man

   6. globes   book

Part B Directions Match the adjectives in Column A with the items from the poem that they describe in Column B. Place the correct letter on the line before each adjective.

Column A	Column B
_____ **1.** paler	**a.** feelers
_____ **2.** relaxed	**b.** underside
_____ **3.** red	**c.** tubes
_____ **4.** tan	**d.** heads
_____ **5.** snaillike	**e.** attic dress
_____ **6.** purple	**f.** webs between the arms
_____ **7.** clear	**g.** rock
_____ **8.** tiny	**h.** water
_____ **9.** pink	**i.** fingers

My Father and Myself Facing the Sun

Directions Listed below are several statements that contain incorrect information about the poem "My Father and Myself Facing the Sun." Underline the incorrect word in each statement. Then write the correct word on the line provided beneath each statement.

1. We are both weak, dark, bright men.

   _____

2. We are both facing into the December sun.

   _____

3. He is the father, and I am his daughter.

   _____

4. There is a river below us.

   _____

5. After a while, there is time to go skiing.

   _____

6. Deer, raccoon, and badger come down to eat.

   _____

7. Gradually, the action begins.

   _____

8. There are seven of our family members present.

   _____

9. At that moment we are all strong and unhappy.

   _____

10. My grandsons are here, too.

   _____

Passports to Understanding

Directions Through her travels, the author of this essay has come to believe many different things about people. Write *Yes* before each statement that represents a belief of the author. Write *No* before each statement that does not represent a belief of the author.

_____ 1. Travel to many destinations is pleasurable.

_____ 2. Americans hear enough different languages in their own country.

_____ 3. No matter how we try, we will always be too different to get very close to people of different backgrounds.

_____ 4. Human beings are more alike than unalike.

_____ 5. Languages collide in America, Europe, and Asia.

_____ 6. The world is populated by people who speak differently.

_____ 7. Travel to many destinations is educational.

_____ 8. Overhearing a language adds to one's understanding of that language.

_____ 9. Different cultures have different philosophies.

_____ 10. Travel can prevent bigotry.

_____ 11. All world cultures are really very much alike.

_____ 12. If we try to understand people of different backgrounds, we may become friends.

_____ 13. What is true anywhere is true everywhere.

_____ 14. One cannot negotiate to buy something if different languages are involved.

_____ 15. Hearing other people's languages increases our perceptions.

The Hundred Secret Senses

Directions Complete each sentence below with a word from the Word Bank.
Each word is used only once.

Word Bank				
four	father	mother	cousin	San Francisco
eighteen	pound	scared	remarry	Jello-O
empress	photo	baby	pennies	turtles

1. The narrator and her sister, Kwan, have the same _____.

2. Jack Yee had immigrated to _____.

3. Olivia's father had _____ children.

4. Olivia's _____ was born in Idaho.

5. Olivia's brother Tommy was a _____ when their father died.

6. The woman called Aunt Betty was really Olivia's mom's _____.

7. Something her father said _____ Olivia for years.

8. Kwan was _____ years old when the family met her.

9. Olivia used to go after _____ her father threw in the wading pool.

10. In the hospital, Olivia ate _____ from her father's food tray.

11. Olivia was afraid her father would send her to the _____.

12. She had killed her pet _____.

13. In the hospital, Mom stared at a _____ of Kwan.

14. Mother said that Olivia's father had treated her like a Chinese _____.

15. Olivia's mother vowed that she would never _____.

Papi Working

Directions Write *True* if the statement is true. Write *False* if it is not true.

_____ 1. The Dominican Republic is in South America.

_____ 2. Julia was a child in the Dominican Republic, although she was born in New York.

_____ 3. The poem has no repeated phrases.

_____ 4. The poem does not have end rhymes.

_____ 5. The poem was written in free verse.

_____ 6. Imagery is the use of words that appeal to the intellect.

_____ 7. The Spanish word for *syrup* is *nada*.

_____ 8. Papi works as a janitor.

_____ 9. Papi seems very sad.

_____ 10. The poem indicates that Papi and the other people prefer the United States to the land of their birth.

_____ 11. Most people mentioned in the poem are not really sick.

_____ 12. The people enjoyed hearing Papi speak Spanish.

_____ 13. The reader is given the idea that Americans pay no attention to clocks.

_____ 14. Papi compares the United States to a pill.

_____ 15. Papi misses his homeland.

The Antelope Wife

Part A Directions Choose the name of the person from the box that each phrase below applies to. Write the abbreviation for the name on the line before each phrase.

_____ 1. Baked sweet bannock

_____ 2. Sawed buttons with a steel instrument

_____ 3. Had a hungry, curious quality

_____ 4. Task was to spy for hidden nests

_____ 5. Had a business in Aberdeen

_____ 6. Bought guinea fowl from a Polish widow

_____ 7. Had a confident smile

_____ 8. Spoke as plainly and slowly as humanly as possible

_____ 9. Owned a small sod and plank house

_____ 10. Had a pliable long waist and graceful neck

_____ 11. Came to the Great Plains and won a teaching certificate

_____ 12. Invented a bore and punch

_____ 13. Had to teach the alphabet

_____ 14. Wore a necklace of bright indigo beads

_____ 15. Made hairpins from bone

> Peace McKnight (PM)
> Peace's father (PF)
> Matilda Roy (MR)
> Scranton Roy (SR)

The Antelope Wife, continued

Part B Directions   Match each item in Column A with the correct phrase in Column B. Write the letters of your answers on the lines provided.

Column A

_____ 1. pliable

_____ 2. mood

_____ 3. style

_____ 4. soldered

_____ 5. mead

_____ 6. carcass

_____ 7. homestead

_____ 8. pungent

_____ 9. abrupt

_____ 10. inevitably

_____ 11. simile

_____ 12. reclusive

_____ 13. suspicion

_____ 14. morel

_____ 15. consumptive

Column B

a. joined together by the melting of a metal

b. home and surrounding land of a family

c. kind of fungus that can be eaten

d. a dead body

e. a figure of speech that makes a comparison using the word *like* or *as*

f. able to bend freely

g. uncertainty; doubt

h. feeling that writing creates

i. sickly

j. tending to withdraw from others

k. certain to happen at some point

l. rude; blunt

m. having a sharp or biting odor

n. an author's way of writing

o. dark-colored drink made of water, honey, malt, and yeast

Unit 7 Review

Part A Directions   Before each statement below, write the letter of the author
or authors described. Many letters will be used more
than once.

_____   1. Read a poem at President Clinton's inauguration

_____   2. Family deaths had big impact on writing

_____   3. Participated in protests against the Vietnam War

_____   4. Writing focus is on English and Spanish in writer's life

_____   5. Japanese American

_____   6. Mixed-blood member of Turtle Mountain Chippewa

_____   7. Often compares items in nature to human world

_____   8. Wrote *Love Medicine*

_____   9. Raised in Dominican Republic

_____   10. Former Poet Laureate of Maryland

_____   11. Won the Christopher Award

_____   12. Formerly a singer and dancer

_____   13. Wrote *The Joy Luck Club*

_____   14. Grew up in an internment camp in California

_____   15. Focuses mostly on joy in writing

a. Richard Rodriguez
b. Lucille Clifton
c. Robert Bly
d. Lawson Fusao Inada
e. Maya Angelou
f. Amy Tan
g. Julia Alvarez
h. Louise Erdrich

Unit 7 Review, continued

Part B Directions   Match each item in Column A with the correct phrase in Column B. Write the letters of your answers on the lines provided.

Column A

_____ 1. ecstasy

_____ 2. fluent

_____ 3. philosophy

_____ 4. acknowledge

_____ 5. consoling

_____ 6. exotic

_____ 7. profile

_____ 8. reticent

_____ 9. perceive

_____ 10. raucous

_____ 11. luminous

_____ 12. anglicized

_____ 13. linguistic

_____ 14. vulnerable

_____ 15. diminutive

Column B

a. very loud, noisy, or disorderly

b. not native to where one is found; mysterious

c. to see; to observe

d. giving off light

e. open to attack; able to be hurt

f. relating to languages or speech

g. able to speak a language very well

h. human head or face seen from a side view

i. familiarly known word or name

j. values, beliefs, attitudes, or concepts of a person or group

k. take notice of

l. intense joy or delight

m. changed to English usage

n. comforting

o. unwilling

Sample Note Cards for a Research Project

Directions Use index cards to take notes for a research project. Study the following sample note cards for a bibliography entry for a book, an encyclopedia, or a magazine or periodical. Note the information included on each card.

1. Write the topic or subtopic at the top of each card.

2. Include all information and punctuation as shown in the sample cards below. Write the last name of the author first. If the name of the author is not known, begin with the next item. Underline titles of books, encyclopedias, and magazines. Use quotation marks around titles of chapters or articles.

3. Write your notes for your research project below each bibliography entry.

Topic: _____
Last name of author, First name of author. Date of publication.
<u>Title of Book</u>. Place of publication: Publisher.

Book Entry

Magazine Entry

Topic: _____
Last name of author, First name of author. "Title of Article."
<u>Title of Magazine</u>. Volume number (Date): Page numbers.

Topic: _____
<u>Title of Encyclopedia</u>, Number of edition, volume number:
Page numbers.

Encyclopedia Entry

Writing Outlines

An outline can be written to organize ideas. Read the sample outline below. This outline presents information included in the About the Author section shown on page 424 of your text. Its two main sections (I and II) include ideas expressed in each paragraph about poet Lucille Clifton. Subtopics and details are listed under each main idea.

Directions   Study this sample outline. Then choose an author from a unit in your textbook. Outline the information given about that person in the About the Author section. The title of your outline will be the author's name. Create a heading (I, II, etc.) to describe the main idea of each paragraph. Subtitles for headings are listed as *A, B, C,* etc. If necessary, other details may be included as *1, 2, 3,* etc. Include all important information. Write your outline on your own paper.

Lucille Clifton

I.   Her Personal Life

     A. Her childhood

        1. Born in New York

        2. Worked at an early age

        3. Enjoyed telling stories

     B. Her later life

        1. Attended college

        2. Formed a theater group

        3. Married in 1958

        4. Had six children

II.   Her Writing Career

     A. Won a poetry contest

     B. Gave a poetry reading in New York

     C. Published "Good Times"

     D. Was a success

        1. Nominated for Pulitzer Prize

        2. Served as poet laureate of Maryland
